PRAISE FOR

MW00532413

"*A perfect how-to to write the perfect mystery! Even seasoned writers might learn a thing or two with this one. The authors lay out the beats and give writers a step-by-step guide on how to write/outline a mystery that will keep readers glued to the page. Highly recommend!!!*"

— NY TIMES BESTSELLING AUTHOR
DARYNDA JONES

"*Inspiring and entertaining, this book provides a useful guide to writing a well-plotted, well-paced, and well-twisted mystery both for beginners and the more experienced writer.*"

— DIANNE FREEMAN, AUTHOR OF THE
AWARD-WINNING COUNTESS OF
HARLEIGH MYSTERIES

DEMYSTIFYING THE BEATS

DEMYSTIFYING THE BEATS

HOW TO WRITE A KILLER BOOK

CAROL POTENZA

JORDYN KROSS   RYLEY BANKS

ERIN KRUEGER

RED REINES, LLC

Published by Red Reines, LLC

website: www.redreines.com

Identifiers: ISBN: 978-1-7363262-7-5 (paperback) | 978-1-7363262-6-8 (ebook)

Proofread: Gilly Wright

Cover: Brandi Doane McCann

CONTENTS

HELLO

We are Jordyn Kross and Carol Potenza. We write fiction and are published authors, both traditionally and indie. Jordyn writes award-winning erotic romance and erotic cozy mysteries, and Carol writes contemporary murder mysteries. In fact, Carol won the Tony Hillerman Prize for her debut mystery, *Hearts of the Missing*.

In addition to writing, we both have analytical backgrounds. Jordyn works in the computer industry developing processes to improve efficiency and providing training on how to do things like make software work the way you want it to. Carol has an extensive background in biochemistry and research, including DNA and genetic engineering. If we ever decided to become supervillains, we'd be unstoppable.

But this work would still be a seed without our critique partners, Ryley Banks, who in her super-secret real life is an editor extraordinaire, and Erin Krueger, researcher of all things and referencer of the historical, hilarious, and obscure.

Four brains. Four avid readers. Four avid writers coming together to solve the mystery of what it takes to make a mystery work.

Writing mysteries provides a unique set of challenges. Writers are told, "Write what you know."

Most of us have experience with romance—love and marriage go together like a horse and carriage—with the requisite HEA (Happily Ever After). If you don't read romance and think we're lying, go to Disneyland and count the number of seven-year-old girls dressed like fairy-tale princesses. HEA is in our DNA.

But how many mystery writers have committed murder? (Put your hand down.) Stolen priceless works of art in a daring midnight heist? Kidnapped a member of the royalty for ransom? How many mystery writers have actually even solved a crime? Sure, lawyers and police officers and retired FBI and CIA agents write books. But there are a lot of us out there who faint at the sight of blood, are allergic to cats, or can research the heck out of the type of gun and ammunition used to kill a victim but have never fired one.

We know, deep in our hearts, that *write what you know* is a metaphor for writing about the shared human condition. But we still don't know if it's okay for a never-before-introduced forensics expert to appear out of the blue in the final scene of a mystery and hand us the lynch-pin piece of evidence that fingers the murderer. (Actually, we do, and no, it's not okay.)

So, we struggled through plotting and writing our mysteries, digging into blogs and books that promised to tell us how to master suspense structure or build unforgettable stories. And while they were helpful, they weren't *that* helpful.

When should the bodies drop? What the heck is a MacGuffin or Chekhov's gun? (Get a clue about these now in our Mystery Dictionary at the end of this book.) Can my sleuth withhold clues or evidence from my reader? (No.)

We also realized that, like romance, there are at least two major protagonists: the sleuth and the villain. They come together over a crime, they spar with each other throughout the body of the story, and in the end, they come together again when "All is Revealed."

Suddenly, in a why-didn't-we-think-of-this-sooner kind of way, we realized, hey, maybe we could do something that would benefit authorkind. Maybe we could write a story structure guide that would be simple enough to give the foundation for driving mysteries from the first clue drop to the *je t'accuse!* Maybe we could inspire you to create your own *Ah-ha!* moments when you put pen to paper (fingers to keyboard?). Maybe we could help you write your mystery novel.

Why?

Because this is a killer book.

YOUR FIRST CLUE

What this book is: A guide for mystery writers of all subgenres.

As we were writing our first mysteries, we came to understand that successful stories have an underlying structure. If any of the engine parts—beats—are missing, unbalanced, or grossly misplaced, problems quickly surface and massive rewrites follow. (Yeah, ask us how we know...) These are not just scene adjustments, but scene abandonment and story restructuring.

No one should have to reinvent the wheel. This book will give you the mystery-building tools you can use over and over again.

What this book isn't: This book will not improve your writing craft.

Your dialogue might still be stilted. Your point of view (POV) might still be shallow. This book is focused solely on the beats that make a mystery work. But don't neglect the other areas of your craft if you want to write a best seller.

Who is in the crosshairs for this book: This book is for beginners who wish to write mysteries and don't quite know how to get started.

This book is for writers who have already drafted their manuscript, know they have a great crime to solve, but something isn't working.

This book is for writers in other genres who wish to add an element of mystery to their story.

So, if you're ready to develop your mystery and don't mind a boatload of mixed metaphors, sloppy clichés, and your grandmother's wise adages...

This book is for you.

Our motives: We were once in your chair, fingers hovering over our keyboard with a mystery we had to write. And no clue how to do it.

As avid readers and viewers of mysteries, surely, we should have known how this worked. And we made HUGE mistakes. So, we investigated what the common elements of a successful mystery are. We've provided examples from books, movies, and television so that you can see these beats, or in some cases the lack of them, in action. And we are sharing our discoveries with you, so we'll have plenty more books and movies to enjoy— maybe with your name on them.

Let's get going.

BEATS ARE GEARS

I f you've been writing for a little while, you've probably heard of "beats." During presentations in writing groups or at conferences, million-copy-selling authors dropped the word so casually. Their audiences nodded so sagely. Their expressions told you they understood exactly how important the beats of the story are. Maybe you, as the newbie, sank down in your seat as panic set in because you wanted to ask for a better explanation but didn't want to look like you *didn't* know.

So, without any smirks of condescension, here is *our* definition of beats.

Beats are the interconnected structural elements of a genre. They are *essential moments* that advance the plot or twist the direction of the story. They can be an action or a reaction, big or small. They can be a single sentence or smeared over several chapters. Some beats are universal to all stories, like introducing the protagonist. Some are specific to the genre, like presenting the crime in a mystery or adhesion of the protagonists in romance.

You've heard the old adage: You have to know the rules (of writing) before you break them?

Listen up, because this is important:

BEATS ARE RULES YOU CANNOT BREAK.

YOU HAVE TO HAVE THEM IN YOUR STORY.

THEIR ORDER MATTERS…to a point.

All the beats, whether universal or specific, must be in the story for it to *work*.

This book is about MYSTERY beats. Not Romance beats or War beats or Western beats. Just Mystery beats.

Are you ready to dive in headfirst? Not yet? Good. We'll get to the mystery beats in a sec. First, let's lay the foundation.

WHODUNIT OR
HOWCATCHEM

I f you want to write a mystery, you probably already have a pretty good idea of what one is, but let's just get it out there so we can agree and proceed.

A mystery is a story where the protagonist (sleuth) is dealing with a puzzling situation (mystery), and the antagonist (villain) is a prominent character. The solution to the mystery, including motive, is presented to the reader in incremental steps, until the very end when the mystery *must* be solved.

There are two overarching types of mysteries: the classic mystery, or *Whodunit*, and an inverted mystery, or *Howcatchem*.

In a Whodunit, the sleuth (and reader) has no clue who the villain is, and the sleuth (and reader) attempts to figure out WHO DUN IT. Get it?

In a Howcatchem, you expose the villain right off the bat. The reader knows from the beginning Whodunit and how it was done, but the sleuth doesn't. The rest of the story is a cat-and-mouse game between the sleuth and the bad guy. The intrigue of the story is following the sleuth as they figure out HOW (to) CATCH thEM.

No matter which story style you write, the beats still work.

TAKING OUT A CONTRACT

Mystery readers have expectations. Don't betray them because they WILL come after you. Maybe not with pitchforks and torches, but with devastating reviews. If you fail to deliver on the promise of a great story, readers will abandon your buy button to search for another book that's guaranteed to get the job done.

What are we talking about? What is this "contract?"

To start, your readers expect a primary mystery. And it must be solved by the end of the story.

This primary mystery draws forth a sleuth: Sherlock Holmes, Precious Ramotswe, or even the Scooby Doo gang.

Is your sleuth likable? Is your sleuth sympathetic or kind of a jerk? Are they admirable and relatable? Do they have demons and problems that interfere with their job? You, as the writer, get to decide.

Now you need an adversary. Who instigated the

mystery, and why? An evil genius with a lair in a volcano who wants to take over the world? A dirty cop who needs money to feed his habit? A bored housewife with a grudge against a neighbor who's been her rival since high school? Again, it's up to you, but don't give away who your villain is unless you are writing a Howcatchem. Let the reader try to figure it out. But don't make it easy!

Your sleuth conducts the investigation centered on a closed circle of suspects who have motive and opportunity. The investigator narrows the pool of suspects by gathering evidence and clues, making deductions based on their past experience.

About that evidence, those clues, and deductions—mystery readers are drawn in by the puzzle that must be assembled to solve the crime. They're searching for the obvious and obscure, the overlooked hints and the red herrings. The evidence must be present. Are they layered in a description? Buried deep in fast-paced dialogue? Or dropped randomly in a list? It's a game you, as the mystery writer, play with the reader.

Writers can leave gaps but must give the reader enough information to make their own deductions—filling in those empty spaces and connecting seemingly unrelated facts. Other mysteries can occur as subplots in your story. These are obstacles or distractions thrown in the way of your sleuth and readers to block them from solving the primary mystery.

Readers derive great satisfaction when all of the clues are given to them, and their deductions parallel that of the sleuth. They want to ferret out the hidden clues, twist them in their brains, and come up with their own —likely wrong—conclusions. Because, when it comes right down to it, they want to be smarter than you, dear writer. But they love to be surprised.

Let's distill this contract down to some Dos and Don'ts.

Do

- Solve the primary mystery. You MUST solve the primary crime by the end of your book. Period.
- Share the clues and evidence with your reader, giving them the opportunity to solve the mystery along with your sleuth.
- Obfuscate the solution. The pleasure is in the puzzle.
- Tie up ALL the *primary* mystery's loose ends.

Don't

- Introduce last-minute characters to complete the puzzle. This includes the villain. That's cheating.
- Omit critical clues—if the detective knows it, the reader needs to know it.
- Justify hiding or omitting clues and evidence by using an unreliable narrator.

- Rely on Deus ex Machina to solve the mystery.

It won't matter how appealing your sleuth is, or how devious a villain you create, or how surprising and original your crime is, if you don't fulfill your reader contract.

The best way to do that is to make sure you have your mystery beats in place.

FOUR ACTS

The three-act structure in stories, books, plays, movies, etc., is classic, going back millennia in oral and written history. It divides the story into three parts: beginning, middle, and end. But an odd thing happens in the application of the three-act structure. We've noticed that in novels and longer films, the middle act is often split in two. They have even been labeled Act II: 1 and Act II: 2. Basically, three acts and four acts are the same thing.

By Royal Edict, we will use a four-act structure for our definition of the beats.

————

The Four Acts

Just like successfully burying a body requires four phases—soak the ground, dig the hole, place the body, fill the hole—a successful mystery has four phases or acts that we've labeled as follows:

Act 1: Setup
Act 2: Fumbling
Act 3: Connecting
Act 4: Solution

Each act has an overarching goal achieved by including the beats—moments that must occur to move a mystery forward. Each act has potential gotchas or pitfalls to avoid. Each of the beats has specific objectives to meet and methods to achieve the beat. We're going to cover all this in detail in the next sections.

Which brings us to the concept of smearing the beat. While we have placed the mystery beats in specific acts, it is possible to add your beats in such a way that the objectives are achieved over several scenes or even several chapters within the act, especially if you're writing a novel-length book.

THE BODY OF THE BOOK

ACT 1 - SETUP

The sleuth and the crime
Your mission is to hook the reader's attention and ground them in the story. The characters you introduce—the sleuth, the villain, the suspects, even the victim—need to be compelling and unique. Compelling characters have flaws and misbeliefs—know them before you proceed. This act is also where you establish the tone. Is this going to be a light, funny, fast-paced read or a dark, brooding blood-fest that will make the reader leave the lights on at night? Begin as you mean to go on.

———

Goal: Propel the sleuth to the crime.

Gotchas:

- Too much backstory or world-building details can kill your pace and bore your readers.
- Failure to introduce the suspects, including the culprit.
- A too-perfect sleuth. Compelling characters have imperfections.

———

Act 1 Beats

Introduce Sleuth and the World

Expose the Crime

Reactions and Complications

Undertaking the Investigation

The first two beats may occur in reverse order if you are doing a Howcatchem. Meaning you might expose your crime and establish your world and then introduce the sleuth. But no matter the order, these objectives should be met in Act 1, even if the LAST thing you do in this act is having your sleuth step out into the world you've created.

INTRODUCE SLEUTH AND
THE WORLD

I s your sleuth a fedora-wearing cigar chewer in today's urban Canada, an abused foster-child-turned-cop in a flying-car future, or a flapper in 1920s Australia with a penchant for handsome men? Whoever they are, you, as the writer, must know them and their world better than your best friend and your own backyard. You get to decide, but their reactions to events must be believable for the character you've created.

———

METHODS AND OBJECTIVES

Establish time and place
Do this from the point of view of your opening character. Using the sleuth, the villain, a witness, or even the victim, establish when and where the story takes place.

Be creative about how you share this information. Use the character's interaction with their environment to provide relevant details. Are they pulling on a sweater? Programming their automatic food machine for a breakfast burrito? Are they at home or work or someplace they shouldn't be?

What are the limitations of the world, especially as they impact your characters? Your time and place will influence what your sleuth can do, what they wear, what they say, and how they say it. In what ways will this complicate the investigation?

Anne Perry's *The Charlotte and Thomas Pitt Series* (1979-2015) includes a Victorian police detective and his upper-class wife. When investigating murders in aristocratic London, Charlotte, with her genteel background, is accepted into the homes and world of people Thomas would never be able to penetrate as a working-class man.

As your story progresses, continue to build the world through your POV characters' eyes.

Create a compelling connection to your sleuth

Sleuths are human (mostly), and we need to present them as such with their strengths and weaknesses clearly evident. The goal is to develop empathy and curiosity in the reader about the sleuth as a person. Creating a rich, three-dimensional protagonist is critical. There must be many facets to their character that can be leveraged for their character arc. Sleuths can be likable... or a monster...or both.

Who are we talking about?

The secret serial killer, clandestine cat burglar, or the brain-eating zombie pathologist. Or *Dexter* (Showtime, 2006-2013), based on the *Darkly Dreaming Dexter* books by Jeff Lindsay. Dexter is a sweet, appealing, and easy-going blood-spatter analyst for the Miami police... Aaannd, he's a psychopathic serial killer with a lust for blood and a defined code of ethics. Dexter became a monster because of the horrific abuse he suffered as a young child and frequently investigates crimes involving child abuse. The viewer relates to this killer character and even cheers him on. Brilliant.

Your sleuth will also need to have a unique skillset useful for solving mysteries. It could be extreme attention to detail. A personality that invites others to share their intimate secrets. A deep knowledge of biochemical poisons. During the opening act, establish the skills they will use to solve this crime.

Who you choose as your sleuth is important because mystery readers are smart. If you decide to make your sleuth own a pastry shop but as the writer you don't know the difference between a macaron and a macaroon, your story might be a did-not-finish (DNF) before the body hits the floor. Details of the sleuth's world matter a great deal to the reader. Know your stuff or do a tremendous amount of research.

. . .

Disrupt the ordinary

Your sleuth exists in their ordinary world. On Tuesday, they bake tarts or attend the morning meeting at the station house. Your job is to give a hint of the ordinary—only a hint, because ordinary often equals boring—and disrupt it. This disruption will be the start of chaos that leads to a crime scene. A crime only they can solve.

Joe Leaphorn in Tony Hillerman's *Dance Hall of the Dead* (1973) is tracking a fly while his chief of police drones on and on about a case on a neighboring reservation. It's not until Leaphorn hears that two boys are missing and a bicycle has been left behind in a pool of blood that he realizes this is not his usual missing person's case.

Ordinary, meet disrupted.

Expose internal and external goals and needs

What's at stake for your characters? Not only around the crime, but in their ordinary world? Often the crime overlaps the sleuth's personal life. Their motivation to solve the crime becomes driven by emotion, even if it's just to prove they are smarter than their antagonist.

In Agatha Christie's *Murder on the Orient Express* (1934), Hercule Poirot's train gets stuck in a snowbank and a body is discovered in a locked sleeping compartment. As the murder becomes more and more impossible to explain, his ego demands he solve the crime before the snow is cleared and his suspects scatter.

Both your villain and sleuth must have an internal

purpose for their actions. And their goals must have a sense of urgency, or ticking clock, associated with them.

But your characters shouldn't be sitting around waiting for the crime to happen (mostly). They should focus on making a living, dealing with relationships, and all the conflicts attached. For the villain, the crime should be a result of their conflicts. For the sleuth, the crime should disrupt their ordinary life.

Maybe your character is a PI and actually *is* sitting around waiting for a crime to occur so he can get a paying gig. You still have to share the why behind his actions. Was he was fired from the police force and if he doesn't get a job soon, he's going to starve and he's already sleeping in his dinky office because his husband kicked him out when he lost his job? Maybe his internal goal is to show his spouse that he can be productive and contribute to the household.

Internal and external goals and needs help create a three-dimensional believable character that readers find compelling.

EXPOSE THE CRIME

The crime is the raison d'être (reason for being) for a mystery. This murder, or this theft, or this kidnapping needs to stand out in your reader's mind. Make it memorable.

———

METHODS AND OBJECTIVES

Put the crime on the page

The only event that is more important than the resolution is the crime. Without the mystery, the story is pointless. The crime should be explosive. It must disrupt the status quo and provoke strong emotions.

The exposure of the crime is going to be either the opening image or a mid act climax, but no later than the end of Act 1. In a Howcatchem, the author should literally show the reader what happened. In a Whodunit, the discovery of the crime should be on the page. These scenes must be visceral and visual. Meaning you want to stab your reader in the feels. Use the five senses—hear, smell, taste, see, touch—to add specific details.

Introduce plausible suspects

Suspects are secondary characters, but you need to convince the reader that some or all of them could be the villain. They must be more fully developed than an extra or a walk-on. Plausible suspects will have had the means, motive, and opportunity, but likely not all three.

You want to get most of these characters on the page and stuck in your reader's mind. They need to be described in sufficient detail that the reader can separate them from other characters if they reappear. You don't want your reader flipping back in the story asking, "Who is this person again?"

But we don't need to know everything about them right away. We'll learn more as the investigation progresses.

It's expected in a cozy or house party mystery that all the suspects are present at the mansion or small town or event—a conference, a creepy carnival, or a beauty pageant. In other subgenres, suspects can be introduced as late as the second act, but no later. Otherwise, there's no time to develop the character. The reader will feel cheated if they don't have time to suspect the suspect who might be the villain. Which leads us to the next objective of this beat.

. . .

Introduce the villain

The villain should be as memorable as the other suspects, but not much more—unless you are writing a Howcatchem. The villain could be introduced right after the exposure of the crime, or later in Act 1, but definitely no later than the end of Act 2. You may even decide to introduce the villain prior to the crime in an interaction with the sleuth or the victim.

REACTION AND
COMPLICATIONS

I n your story world, your sleuth is a real person with real feelings and a real life outside of solving crimes, unless they are a robot—and, sorry, that doesn't get you off the hook. They have a past and all the emotional history that comes with. They have a present which may not be conducive to crime solving. Even the seemingly mundane issue of vacating their apartment for a few days for maintenance can provide a complication and distraction for your protagonist.

As a real person, they need to have a reaction to the crime. Revulsion, empathy, intrigue—something.

———

METHODS AND OBJECTIVES

Emotionally engage the sleuth

The detective needs to be emotionally engaged with

the mystery. Even if the sleuth is a professional assigned to the case, they should be personally motivated to solving the crime.

If your sleuth is an amateur, she might be a nosy parker like Jessica Fletcher (*Murder, She Wrote*, 1984-1996) who is looking for more material for her latest crime novel. Or the sleuth could be a suspect who needs to clear themselves. Perhaps they were connected to the victim personally and they want justice.

Whatever it is, if your sleuth is emotionally invested, even if it's just their ego, your reader will be more invested as well.

Introduce private life

The reaction to the events of the story will be based on who your detective is and what's going on in their life.

Not only is the private life subplot useful for connecting to the crime, but it helps create a fully developed character. It can also be useful for adding complications to the investigation. For example, it's hard to go sleuthing if you're toting around your two-year-old grandson or a half-grown puppy that isn't house-trained. Talk about the potential to contaminate a crime scene!

While a personal story can bond the reader to a sleuth, it doesn't have to be a major part of the plot, especially if you're writing a series. Rarely on the TV show *Law & Order* (1990-present) do the detectives or attorneys have a personal connection to their cases. But we do learn about the characters' parents, their love lives, and even their health.

Bonus: if you, the writer, are creating a series, personal issues don't have to be resolved by the end of the book like the primary mystery. They can be carried into the next book. The private life subplot becomes an emotional hook for the reader and creates a bond that will have them anticipating the next release. Talk about smearing the beats.

Introduce supporting characters

It's not mandatory to have a partner or a team, but, in general, it's bad to leave your character alone for too long. When left to their own devices, our characters start rambling in narrative, and it can lead to a lack of action or conflict. Give your sleuth a sidekick, a partner, a mentor, or even a frenemy they can use as a sounding board.

Allies can provide complications, insight, or additional information. Maybe your sleuth's friend happens to work at the motor vehicle department and does a sneaky search for them, or your sleuth is new to the community and finds a neighbor who knows everything about everybody.

As the story, or series, progresses, continue to flesh out these side characters. Give them their own backstory, flaws, and inner and outer goals.

UNDERTAKING THE INVESTIGATION

The investigator is in a race. When that pistol fires (at your victim), the runners are off. The goal is to win the race, set the record, get the gold medal—solve the crime. A sense of urgency needs to be established to propel the story forward. Stakes and a ticking clock work in tandem to compel your reader to stay up late and keep turning the page.

———

METHODS AND OBJECTIVES

Commit to investigate

The story is dead if there is no investigator. Getting your sleuth to commit to solving the mystery is the most important thing in this beat. Going back to our runner analogy, if they don't show up for the race, the stakes and the ticking clock are rather pointless.

How does your sleuth express their commitment? Do they start an evidence board in their office? Maybe they investigate their first clue. It could even be a conversation with their sidekick about why they have to figure out Whodunit or Howcatchem.

However you write it, make it clear that the protagonist is tied to resolving the crime, even if they don't want to be. They might still win the *Miss Congeniality* (2000) award in the end.

Set the stakes

What does the detective have to lose if the criminal is not identified? Or does the investigator have something gain by solving this crime? What does the villain have to lose if the sleuth solves the crime? What do the victims—assuming they aren't dead—or their families have to lose?

Stakes can change over the course of the story.

In their true crime novel, *The Monster of Florence* (2008), authors Douglas Preston and Mario Spezi start out exploring a series of unsolved murders in Italy. But as they poked and probed into old case files, they discovered huge mistakes and extreme negligence by the police and the justice system. Suddenly, Preston and Spezi are accused of obstruction of justice and of being accomplices. Hoo, boy, with their physical safety at risk, did their initial stakes change!

Financial security can also be compelling reasons for your sleuth or your villain to act. For example, the detective who is going to be fired or demoted is risking financial security if they don't solve the crime.

Love and belonging are common stakes for a sleuth in a cozy. What if their daughter or cousin or other dear family member stands accused? They're motivated to solve the crime as if they themselves are under scrutiny.

Self-esteem or possibly self-actualization is what is at stake for Sherlock Holmes. His identity is tied to his ability to be the best detective and to outwit every deceptive tactic the villain employs. Can you imagine his therapy bill if he failed?

Specify a deadline

Deadlines are great motivators to keep your readers turning the pages. Why can't this crime become a cold case? How long can the detective commit to finding the criminal? Can they stop a serial killer before they commit another murder?

When your sleuth's job at the bakery is threatened because the owner has been arrested for a murder he didn't commit, it adds delicious tension. And with a buried box kidnapping, the ticking clock pounds in the reader's ears.

Expand the pool of suspects

Introduction of suspects doesn't have to wait for the crime to be exposed. Witnesses and most suspects should be identified within the first act. Witnesses can give initial statements of fact: what they saw or heard.

Make sure the sleuth is asking witnesses and suspects questions to set the investigation in motion. "How did you know the victim?" "Do you know if the victim had any enemies?" "Where were you at the time of the crime?"

Witnesses and suspects relay information to the sleuth that advances or misdirects the investigation. And those witnesses? Don't forget them as possible suspects.

A word of caution: don't introduce too many generic characters or the reader will become confused. Characters need to be unique and memorable to live in the reader's mind.

ACT 2 - FUMBLING

Fumbling—in the dark
When we say fumbling, we mean that the sleuth is as deeply in the dark as the reader. Both need to figure out the whys and whatfors of the crime.

The goal in Act 2 is to gather evidence and information about the mystery: the victim, the suspects, and the possible witnesses. Little unconnected clues are found but have no meaning. The picture is incomplete.

In this act, your sleuth is more reactive than proactive. It's not until later acts that your sleuth realizes what is important, what is unrelated, and what might still be missing.

———

Goal: Build the foundation for solving the crime.

Gotchas:

- The investigation goes too smoothly.
- Investigation scenes don't produce any results, not even crumbs.
- Events occur rapid fire, and there is no reflection time for the sleuth or the reader.

———

Act 2 Beats

Investigations and Interrogations
Develop the Sleuth
Motives and Lies
Dire Disruption

The beats of Act 2 can be distributed across the act except for the dire disruption which should occur as the midpoint climax of the story (end of Act 2). The investigation will lead to interrogations of potential suspects and witnesses. Suspects will begin to reveal their motives but should also conceal details with lies. While the investigation is progressing, the sleuth's personal life continues to intrude. The goal is to make the path to the solution winding and bumpy and not at all easy.

INVESTIGATIONS AND INTERROGATIONS

The crime has been exposed. We've met the sleuth and possibly the villain. Now it's time to do the work. Show your reader how your sleuth approaches solving the mystery.

METHODS AND OBJECTIVES

Make a plan

By the end of Act 1, your sleuth has committed to solving the crime. What will they do next? It could be as simple as determining who they want to investigate and questioning them. Or it could involve contacting experts and putting their special skills to use. Perhaps they decide they're going to bake some cookies and worm their way into the reclusive neighbor's house for a surreptitious search. The point of the plan is to identify what they don't know and how they are going to find out.

. . .

Gather information

The moment the sleuth is aware of the crime, they start the investigation. What are the particulars of the mystery?

The crime defines the path of the investigation. Is it an abduction or a burglary or a cold case? What is the method? The method of the crime will inform the sleuth of potential suspects. What were the skills required to commit the crime? Where and when did it happen? Is it a locked sleeping compartment or a cornfield? The sleuth evaluates who had access to the location of the crime.

Interview witnesses, family members, and the cops on the beat. Elicit information that leads your sleuth to the next person, who then adds another bit of information and maybe drops another name.

In Joanna Fluke's *Chocolate Chip Cookie Murder* (2013), the second act is filled with the sleuth interviewing suspects and possible witnesses—the information she gathers in one interview leads directly to the next interview, then the next, and so on. Very linear.

It doesn't have to be that way. Private detectives might have a list of people to interview and do it in a more scattershot manner. Don't forget to add in a pinch of hunch and intuition, keeping in mind a little goes a long way. And not all your witnesses and suspects should be forthcoming. The answers to your sleuth's question might be clues or red herrings or outright lies sprinkled between their truths.

The tone of the questions will depend on the subgenre. Professionals take statements and interview witnesses. Cozy sleuths might chat with a suspect over coffee. Some of your suspects have already been on the page. Others still need to be introduced. Meet with your suspects and witnesses from the first act. Introduce the final suspects through the second act. But make sure your villain is mixed in and doesn't stand out because he's twirling a Snidely Whiplash mustache or looks like Boris and Natasha. Hide the villain under the bushel where his light doesn't shine...for now.

One more thing. What evidence is present and what is missing? Sometimes the best clues are the details that aren't present but should be!

Evaluate

A lot has happened in Act 1. As part of creating a plan to investigate and gather information, it's important to evaluate what was learned. A great way to do this is a discussion with their team, a sidekick, or partner. Recap to bring everyone up to speed on the evidence and suspects.

It's easy to smear this beat. Evaluation will be an ongoing effort throughout your story. Watson frequently asks Sherlock, "How did you know that?" Then Sherlock details all the information he gathered to come to a particular conclusion. Mysteries tend to be complex, with multiple suspects, with multiple motives, and includes truth, lies, and misdirection.

Fumbling can get messy. Details can be missed. Somewhere in the second act, remind your reader what they might have missed and how the sleuth will go forward with that information.

DEVELOP THE SLEUTH

It's time for your reader to get to know your sleuth even better. What makes your sleuth worry at night? What's your sleuth's backstory? How does their fear, beliefs, or value system complicate the investigation?

———

METHODS AND OBJECTIVES

Complicate the sleuth's personal life

Writers are monsters, so we are PERFECT for concocting horrible obstacles our characters must confront. Easy investigations, sleuths whose personal lives are perfect, and villains who tell the truth make for boring stories.

The private life subplot introduced in Act 1 needs to reappear. Whatever it is, it must move your story along.

Connect it or intertwine it with the main plot, even if the sleuth's calm personal life creates the perfect sharp contrast with the chaos of solving the crime (*Fargo*, 1996).

Add or progress subplots

Another way to show us who your sleuth is and to make their life complicated is to introduce another subplot different from the one introduced previously. This could be a secondary mystery that on the surface appears to be completely unrelated to the original. Or may actually be an entire red herring on its own. Perhaps a romantic interest makes an appearance. Whatever it is, the subplot(s) should uncover layers of character in the detective.

Display sleuth's skills

Your sleuth has a particular style and set of skills that make their way of navigating the investigation unique. Sherlock observes the minute details others fail to notice. Columbo appears to be friendly, bumbling, and forgetful. The two characters couldn't be more disparate in personalities, but they have a similar skill set.

In Tana French's *Into the Woods* (2007), she uses her sleuth's past as a kidnapping survivor to investigate a crime extremely similar to the one he experienced as a child. Joanna Schaffhausen's debut police procedural *The Vanishing Season* (2017) introduces a police officer sleuth who was the only known victim of a serial killer to survive—and there's a serial killer on the loose! Both sleuths have a very special skill set that makes them perfect for the crimes presented in their respective stories. Contrast this with a cozy sleuth who uses a likable personality, personal connections, and in some cases, their weaknesses—like not being able to drive or cook—to acquire information from witnesses and suspects. During the second act, their skills and style should become obvious.

Increase the conflict

Conflict is the basis of story. If there is no struggle, if nothing's at stake, there's no reason to keep reading. Internal conflict reveals flaws or misbeliefs, increasing the empathy and realism of your character.

Your sleuth could be attracted to a suspect. Do they pursue the romance? Or do they follow the clues, even if it means putting that handsome man behind bars?

External conflict can occur between your character and the environment. This could include societal norms, culture, natural elements, or even technology. We gave an example earlier of the historical mystery limiting where the sleuths could go in the course of their investigation. In Carol Potenza's *Hearts of the Missing* (2018), Police Sergeant Nicky Matthews struggles to solve a murder as an outsider in a tight-knit Native American community, sometimes even fighting against the culture.

Between the characters themselves, there should be

competing goals. Suspects and villains have something to hide, which is in direct opposition to your sleuth's mission of discovering the truth.

Conflict is an excellent tool to keep the reader interested and avoid the dreaded muddy middle.

MOTIVES AND LIES

Everybody lies. Especially your characters. Your sleuth will be deluged with truths, but in the middle of all of that—lies. There will be more than one suspect with a motive. Will they hide or over-share to conceal the truth? Consider the personalities of these secondary, but critical, characters as you decide what they confess. Give them a reason to lie, or to kill, and not share their alibi. Keep your reader guessing.

————

METHODS AND OBJECTIVES

Witnesses withhold

You mean your suspects don't answer with the whole truth and nothing but the truth?

Shocking.

Your suspects are in your book for a reason. They

have a motive to perpetrate the crime. They have a reason to break the law. They have specific beliefs about themselves—that they're a good person, that they're an upstanding citizen, that they're trustworthy. But their true motives may be abhorrent to family and friends. Their motivations could contradict who they believe themselves to be. To admit it internally is painful. But to admit it out loud would destroy them.

In the stage play *An Inspector Calls* (J.B. Priestly, 1945), all the suspects are introduced at an English manor dinner party. Characters are established, a loving and prosperous family shown, and everyone is happy until a police inspector arrives. He interrogates each family member about the death of a destitute, pregnant young woman. The truths established in the first act are then peeled away in painful layers to get to the under-lying rot. These people don't want the ugliness of their souls exposed because it paints them in a terrible light.

Suspects lie

During early interrogations, the sleuth doesn't know enough about the crime to distinguish a lie from the truth. Suspects complicate the investigation by impli-cating other people for reasons, including revenge, petti-ness, or their misperception of the truth.

In *Knives Out* (2019), multiple suspects in the death of patriarch Harlan Thrombey overhear loud and contentious arguments between Harlan and some of the family members the night he died. But greed for his money and legacy drive them to reveal this information only to implicate others—even their siblings—because if Harlan was murdered by a rival, their inheritance is forfeit and the accusers get more.

Lies will lead the investigator to the Fast Fail in Act 3.

Everyone is motivated

Motivation is similar to stakes. The more fundamental the motivation is (think Maslow's hierarchy of needs), the more compelling it will be, both for your sleuth and for your reader. Your suspects will hide their motivations. Your sleuth will uncover them.

Make sure your villain has a strong motivation downplayed by their alibi. Include other suspects likely to have done the deed. If the villain's motivation is lackluster, it might steal the thunder from your big reveal.

In a cozy, the victim usually "needs killing," meaning they are such an awful person it's almost expected that people would want them out of their lives. But usually only one character will be desperate enough or angry enough to actually poison the pudding.

Alibis abound

Suspects should provide alibis. A suspect may have a motive to commit the crime, but did they have the means?

As part of the initial interrogations, your sleuth asks the suspects, "Where were you on the night of January fifth between the hours of eight and midnight?" or some version of that.

Some will tell the truth, some will lie. No matter what, dubious alibis need to be confirmed or disproved to whittle down who could have done the crime. If alibis are weak—"I was watching TV by myself"—then your sleuth and reader must sift through more clues to arrive at the solution.

DIRE DISRUPTION

The dire disruption will be at the very end of Act 2 and is the story's midpoint climax. This is the situation encountered by your characters that changes everything. It should be vivid and memorable and compel your readers to turn the page.

The methods and objectives we are providing below are a buffet of dire disruptions. Use one or more of these or create your own.

———

METHODS AND OBJECTIVES

Attack on the investigator

The sleuth is getting too close to solving the crime, so they must also be eliminated. This could be a physical attack, an attack on their reputation, or other disruption of their investigation.

In M.C Beaton's *The Quiche of Death* (2003), a suspect attacks the cozy sleuth, Agatha Raisin, because she's close to uncovering his criminal past, which actually had nothing to do with the murder. It's a dire disruption that also functions as a red herring.

Primary suspect disappears/second body drop

Everything is funneling down to a single suspect— the clues, the evidence, the accusations. You've got your villain—but they disappear. Or become the second victim. The removal or disappearance should be dramatic and unexpected.

In Jordyn Kross's *Dirty Daisy* (2021), the primary suspect threatens the sleuth, Mikaela "Mike" Mitchell. But before they can be brought in for questioning, they're found drowned. As a result, the focus of Mike's investigation shifts.

Throw in a new complication or hurdle

Plot twist! This is your time to shine as an author. Add a complication or a barrier to success that seems insurmountable to your sleuth. Make them suffer. This isn't a minor hiccup. It's a mountain or a crater specific to your character. It will have your reader turning the page to find out how they overcome it, because there is no possible way the sleuth can succeed now.

In the *Psych* (2006-2014) episode *The Spellingg Bee*, the sleuth needs his father to analyze a clue. His dad refuses to help until the sleuth finishes building a doghouse he started in eighth grade, fifteen years earlier.

Raise the stakes

Things need to get Dire, with a capital D. If the sleuth is trying to clear a relative of the crime, arrest the relative. If your sleuth was trying to solve the mystery to save their job, fire or suspend them.

In Tyora Moody's *Deep Fried Trouble* (2013), retired widow, Eugeena Patterson, is pulled into solving her ex-best-friend's murder when Eugeena's prodigal daughter is implicated. Eugeena must find her daughter before the police do.

Hot lead possible

Your sleuth becomes aware of a person or information that seems to change everything. The plan they had, the suspicions they held, are imploded like an old casino on the Las Vegas Strip. They must completely reorient themselves and search for the culprit in a different direction.

In *Ms. Fisher's Modern Murder Mysteries* (2019-21) episode *Seasoned Murder,* the murder victim's wife reveals her explosive temper after a whispered conversation with another suspect, which redirects the focus of the investigation.

. . .

Clear one of the suspects

You've arrested or accused one of your suspects. All the evidence, the witness statements, motive, and opportunity point directly to this despicable villain. They're in jail, awaiting trial. And then there's another murder with the exact same modus operandi. Or forensics come back, and the DNA doesn't match. Or a witness recants.

WHAT IS GOING ON? Welp, you focused on the wrong person.

Time to reassess your case.

ACT 3 - CONNECTING

Connections—danger and enlightenment

Act 3 starts off as a reaction to the Dire Disruption that occurred at the end of Act 2. The sleuth is knocked off their original plan and must regroup. There are new facts to consider, perhaps a new crime, or the disappearance of a suspect, but whatever happened, they must react.

The villain is going to react as well, doing their best to capitalize on that disruption. Secondary characters may be less willing to help with the investigation. Red herrings lead the investigator toward the wrong conclusion, and their personal life is going to have a similar low point. The end result is that your sleuth's job gets more difficult and more urgent.

———

Goal: Fumbling is over, and the clues and evidence are becoming crystal clear. Or are they?

Gotchas:

- Accidental reveal of the villain due to a mishandling of clues and red herrings.
- Lack of conflict and risk can bore your reader.
- Misguided impulse to introduce last minute suspects or Deus ex Machina.

———

Act 3 Beats
   Stonewalled
   Missteps
   Whittle Suspects
   Fast Fail

You can bounce back and forth between the first three beats in this act, so they might not occur in order. But the Fast Fail will be your Act 3 climax.

STONEWALLED

The Dire Disruption forces the sleuth to pause and alter their original plan. They are in danger. They feel self-doubt. They lost an ally. But they must create a new plan because they are still committed to solving the crime. Maybe even more so. The villain will be adjusting and replanning and desperately trying to stop the sleuth at every turn. The sleuth may seek advice from a mentor as they adjust to this new situation.

———

METHODS AND OBJECTIVES

Villain blocks or misdirects the investigation

The villain may be laying false clues or putting others under suspicion.

In one of P.D. James's Edgar-nominated novels, the

murderer actually hires a PI to investigate his son's apparent suicide. When the investigator gets too close to the solution, the murderer then fires the PI.

More investigation and interviews

In this act, the sleuth is driven by insight. They have identified conflicts in the witness statements, holes in the investigation, or more evidence comes to light. Now the investigation is driven by knowledge, not by the lack of knowledge. Your sleuth knows what they don't know —even if they're wrong—and is actively pursuing the facts. But no one is making it easy for them.

One of the witnesses directly contradicts another's alibi. But who's telling the truth? Or your witness is only answering the question as asked, concealing vital information.

In the television show *Law & Order* (*Standoff*, 2000), the detective asks a witness for a list of gang members present in the prison's rec room at the time the victim was shanked. She provides him *exactly* what he asked for, omitting the culprit who was not a gang member.

Sleuth and villain clash

The sleuth and the villain will be in an escalating conflict even though the villain is still unknown in the case of a Whodunit. Or the villain may taunt the sleuth, especially in the case of a Howcatchem. Because the sleuth is making connections and moving toward the truth, the villain is going to use every bit of power they have to block the investigation.

Villains may leverage their influence around the sleuth's personal life, or in one of the subplots, to pull the focus away from the primary mystery entirely.

Consider the relationship of your villain to your sleuth and create unique barriers for your investigator to overcome.

MISSTEPS

The path to the solution is filled with missteps, and right now your sleuth is headed toward a Fast Fail. They are obsessively working toward the correct solution, taking greater risks to the point their actions could be unethical or immoral.

Your sleuth is going to have moments of insight about overlooked clues and clarity about motives. A picture of the crime will start to form. But along with the clarity will come pressure. The stakes are raised. The ticking clock is getting louder. They are going to lose their footing or even lose an ally.

In *The Hounds of Baskerville* episode of *Sherlock* (2010-2017), Sherlock drugs his sidekick John Watson to prove to himself he's on the right track. John frowns on this unethical behavior.

Ally lost.

METHODS AND OBJECTIVES

Return to clues

A lot of information was available during acts one and two when the crime was exposed. But the sleuth was fumbling in the dark. Unimportant details must be revisited to identify gaps in the investigation, missed clues, or misinterpretations. Unfortunately, they may jump to the wrong conclusion.

To play fair with readers, it's important to drop hints for each critical clue three times. Early, middle, and late in the story. The drops can be obvious, buried, or seemingly irrelevant. But by repeating the hints, the reader will declare, "I should have known!" at the resolution.

In Rudolfo Anaya's *Zia Summer* (1996), amateur PI Sonny Baca's cousin is ritually killed, and he's searching for the culprit. He reviews the clues with his friends and police contact at a baseball game. Jumping to the wrong conclusions, he runs headlong into the Fast Fail and accuses the wrong person.

Hidden motives revealed

Suspects and stakeholders lie. Your sleuth is beginning to see through the deceptions. A revelation of a hidden motive may seem like an *Ah-ha!* moment. The reader needs to believe as strongly as the sleuth that now we're getting somewhere. This is the piece of the puzzle we were missing.

In Michael Connelly's legal mystery, *The Lincoln*

Lawyer (2005), the defense attorney Mickey Haller is hired by a high-profile client arrested for a horrific crime. An overlooked parking ticket received outside a murdered woman's home reveals the sinister motive for the client to hire Haller. That murder sent another of Haller's clients to prison.

Villain thwarts the sleuth

Thwarts. A great underused word and it's what your villain is going to do to your sleuth. The culprit sees the progress being made. Feels the pressure of exposure increasing. And it compels them to take action. This might be in the form of planting of false clues, the instigation of chaos in the sleuth's personal life, or even setting up the sleuth as a suspect.

David Baldacci's Howcatchem, *Absolute Power* (1997), begins with a murder committed by the President of the United States. As the sleuth edges closer to revealing the crime, the bad guys attack his daughter, put her in the hospital, and then try to kill her a second time.

For a moment, the villain has the upper hand, and the sleuth is scrambling.

WHITTLE SUSPECTS

The investigation is gaining momentum and the clues are coming together. The sleuth's confidence is increasing as their efforts prove fruitful. Revisiting the earlier clues produced insights, and suspects are being cleared.

————

METHODS AND OBJECTIVES

Unrecognized clues identified

It's time to dig deep into those clues from the previous acts. The sleuth revisited them, but what did they reveal? Did unexpected lab results come back? Was a red herring really red or was it the path to the solution? Earlier subtle clue drops that only the savviest and most suspicious of readers would have caught are exposed as real evidence.

In the *iZombie* (2015-2019) episode, *Brother, Can You Spare a Brain*, a sleuth recognizes that the raised platform in the victim's loft changes the height requirements for the killer.

Suspects cleared or eliminated

As the story moves closer to the end, the pool of suspects continues to dwindle due to new revelations, forensic analysis, or a shameful alibi revealed. Or the sleuth could analyze the timeline again with new information and recognize that a suspect actually has an alibi or appears to.

Add interest to the story by clearing the most likely suspect with evidence. Or even make them the next victim.

In *Queens of Mystery* (2019-present), episode *Death by Vinyl First Chapter*, clues point to the band manager or possibly the drummer as the murderer of the lead singer in an 80s New Wave band. One suspect is eliminated, and one is cleared when the real killer takes out a suspect in front of a witness.

Sleuth gains control

The sleuth is moving quickly to a satisfying solution. They have overcome barriers put into place by the villain and their risky behavior is paying off.

But their control is an illusion.

They are formulating the method with which they

will thwart the villain (NOT) and solve the crime. The sleuth thinks they are winning with their skills. They know exactly what to do next, driving quickly toward a conclusion.

In the *Harry Wild* (2022-present) episode *Samurai Plague Doctors Kill for Kicks*, the sleuth thinks she's gained control and solved the mystery when she has the primary suspect arrested. (Nope). Now she's the target.

This beat is the high that will make the Fast Fail even more painful.

FAST FAIL

The Fast Fail is the dark, all-is-lost beat of your mystery.

The sleuth was flying high, figured everything out, had a clear picture and a likely suspect in their crosshairs. But it's all smoke and mirrors.

They accuse! They arrest! They are WRONG!

It can be a great reason for your character to arc or grow as a person, to force your sleuth to confront a wound or misbelief. It's personally and emotionally very painful.

————

METHODS AND OBJECTIVES

Accusation of an innocent

The sleuth is prepared for the denouement. It's time

to confront the villain and explain how the mystery occurred and collect the accolades.

But they're wrong. Epically wrong.

The more wrong and exposed, and the bigger the fallout from this failure, the more memorable the story. They might accuse someone powerful, someone who could cost them their job, or go after someone who was actually their ally, ruining a relationship they had come to depend on.

In *Murder Mystery* (2019), the married amateur sleuths stand accused of murder. With the stakes high they evade the police and work to find the real murderer. Just when they think they have it figured out they call the detective assigned to the case to accuse their greatest ally, but...(deleted spoiler here). As a result, they lose all credibility.

All is lost personally and/or professionally

The dark moment can revolve around the personal life subplot or their professional career. A risky or unethical action they took earlier comes back to bite them. Their reaction could cause them to question their commitment to solving the crime.

However you create the circumstances to torture your sleuth, it's a gut punch that forces them to change their direction or methodology.

In Tracy Clark's *Broken Places* (2018), a witness in the murder of a beloved priest regains consciousness and is ready to be questioned. A solution to the crime is near.

Then, the officer guarding this witness is pulled away by an emergency, and the killer gains access to the hospital room, setting up the sleuth for a crime. As a result, the sleuth may lose her Private Investigator's license and go to jail.

This beat is the last major turning point before the sleuth solves the crime.

ACT 4 - SOLUTION

Solution—to the mystery
The clearest learning moment is when you're absolutely wrong.

The Fast Fail at the end of Act 3 was a moment of clarity for your sleuth. Once again, they must apply a fresh perspective to the clues and evidence. The urgency to solve the crime before something else happens is increasing.

However you conclude the mystery, it must be solved, and it must be supported by the clues and evidence provided in the previous acts.

———

Goal: Solve the primary mystery

Gotchas:

- Failure to tie up all your loose threads leaving dangling clues. (Which is much worse than dangling participles.)
- Leaving the primary mystery unsolved. (*You* will be your reader's next victim.)

———

Act 4 Beats

Reevaluate

Revelation

Final Battle

Resolution

REEVALUATE

Your sleuth is going to take action during this beat. They recover from the defeat of the Fast Fail and their sense of urgency to correctly solve the crime is high. The sleuth believes the villain is an immediate threat or the clock is running out. They can't be wrong again. They must refocus, reconnect with their allies, and create the final plan of action.

METHODS AND OBJECTIVES

Clarify the clues and eliminate red herrings

Your sleuth gained clarity from a false solution. Some detail about a clue is going to come sharply into focus.

In *Knives Out* (2019), a blood drop on a shoe zooms in importance to the size of an arterial blood spatter.

It's time to tie up some of your red herrings. Whether

you explain them at the end or throughout the fourth act, you must account for all of them.

The *Birds of a Feather* episode of *Murder, She Wrote* (1984-1996), the wife of the victim is seen coming in through a back door, negating her alibi. But this red herring was never explained. Talk about ruffling viewer's feathers!

You also don't have permission to introduce last minute clues or evidence that—voilà—solves the case.

Secrets exposed

Characters lie for a variety of reasons, but the motive must be compelling. If your reader follows your story for more than two hundred and fifty pages, the villain's motive can't be, "I felt like it."

The clarification of means, motive, and opportunity will uncover a secret, putting the sleuth on the correct path. When the villain becomes aware of this exposure, the risk to the sleuth increases.

In Dianne Freeman's *A Lady's Guide to Etiquette and Murder* (2018), the sleuths present sketches to a couple and learn that a gentleman is not who he claims to be. This triggers a reevaluation of all the clues.

Identify holes

Knowing the truth and proving the truth can be miles apart. Just because your sleuth knows who did it, doesn't mean they can prove it.

In *My Cousin Vinny* (1992), when Vinny asks Lisa, "Are you shuw-ah? How could you be so shuw-ah?" Vinny already knows—he has the photographic evidence. But he's missing the other metallic mint green General Motors car. So, he sends the sheriff to fill the hole.

REVELATION

The reevaluation and revelation are going to be woven together like the DNA in your evidence. The sleuth fills holes, confronts liars—possibly the villain—and uncovers the mechanisms that were used to execute the crime.

———

METHODS AND OBJECTIVES

Confrontation

The confrontation can take on different emotional angles depending on how you let it play out. The sleuth could confront the culprit or someone who is lying and intentionally or unintentionally protecting the villain. However it plays out, this confrontation needs to be imbued in conflict. The action and emotion are escalating. This is a skirmish before the final battle.

In *Mystery Road* (2018) season one, *Gone*, the detective confronts a witness who has been withholding critical information for a decade. When she finally divulges the truth, the detective knows who has masterminded all the recent crimes.

Urgency

Unlike real cases, your sleuth can't let the case go cold. Something pushes them forward, dragging them down the path to solve the mystery.

The statute of limitations is nearly up. Their vacation is over, and their return flight leaves in a matter of hours. Or the train will pull into the station, or the killer will strike again.

It doesn't matter as long as it's appropriate for your story and is making the clock beat so loudly your sleuth has to scream to be heard over it.

Acquire necessary evidence

You are not allowed to have a missing piece in your puzzle. Your sleuth must track down the final details to prove their solution is correct. They might return to the scene of the crime. They could revisit an expert to get a new facet or a twist on an already examined clue. This isn't finding a last-minute piece to the puzzle: it's taking an existing piece, spinning it around and trying it in a new location. The clue already existed, but now it takes on new meaning.

Paul Holes covers the true crime case of the Golden State Killer, who was active from 1974 to 1986, in his book, *Unmasked* (2022). Using existing DNA evidence, previously unmatched to anyone, investigators submitted samples to commercial DNA databases almost twenty years after the crimes stopped. Matches to distant relatives enabled them to deduce the identity of this monster.

Threats

Your sleuth is getting uncomfortably close to the solution and the villain will add another layer of threat, either foreshadowed or actual. The solution will not come fast enough to save the day. Threats will add to the sense of urgency in this beat.

In Carol Potenza's *The Third Warrior* (2021), a young boy is kidnapped by the killer in a last-ditch effort to escape his crimes. But it's this new threat that finally reveals them and their underlying motives. Now the villain's only escape is to eliminate the sleuth —permanently.

The sleuth's actions in this beat will pave the way to the final battle.

FINAL BATTLE

The final battle is what your reader has been breathlessly waiting for. The sleuth will confront the villain—and it will epic, right? And the solution is clear as crystal. Only your sleuth can solve this mystery, conquer the villain, and win the day.

————

METHODS AND OBJECTIVES

Resolution of subplot

Resolution of one of the subplots is a great opportunity to show your character's arc. That's the growth they have made over the course of this story. If they were about to be fired for not being a team player, the subplot resolution could revolve around them working with their team. It's time to start tidying up the loose ends. The subplot resolution should relate to the success the sleuth has in the final confrontation.

In Jacqueline Winspear's *Maisie Dobbs* (2003), a woman's loss of her first love, a war vet, who she doesn't believe committed suicide sets in motion Maisie's investigation into a retreat for soldiers suffering battle fatigue. The investigation gives Maisie the courage to face her own wartime loss. The resolution ties both the investigative plot and Maisie's personal subplot together in a fine and brilliant bow.

Final confrontation

In the final confrontation, the sleuth is going to use their special skills to triumph over the villain. This confrontation needs to be memorable and satisfying for the reader.

Consider carefully where this confrontation takes place. Any old sidewalk in your town is not going to cut it. Where is an emotionally laden location that will elevate the battle?

How is the battle going to play out? A battle of the wits? A physical challenge? Or a psychological trap?

What format will best showcase your sleuth's skills and ratchet up the risk?

Who is the audience for the battle? Is this going to be a public outing or a personal tête-à-tête?

Each decision you make should intensify the scene.

In the *Hinterland* (2013-2016) episode *Devil's Bridge*, the detective confronts the killer in her childhood church while she's murderously attacking the priest. During this final battle, another death is revealed, and the killer's rage is redirected.

The final battle is the scene that will decide whether your reader is going to recommend your book in a great review or never read anything you write again.

No pressure.

RESOLUTION

The Resolution is your closing. It should leave your readers with a sense of completion and satisfaction and perhaps a little bit of anticipation if you're writing a series. It's a great time to answer any questions that were asked in the subplots if they haven't been resolved. This is also the moment to foreshadow the future.

If you look at your mystery as an experiment, the opening was the presentation of the question: Whodunit or Howcatchem. The next two acts are all about gathering data, defining methods, and obtaining documentation and feedback. This final act is the test—the final battle—and the analysis of the results. Together, they deliver on the contract to satisfy the reader.

———

METHODS AND OBJECTIVES

Final details explained

As the mystery was resolved in the final battle, there were likely details that didn't get fully explained. Walk the reader through the solution. Resolve any remaining subplot. Clear up any lingering red herrings. (See any episode of BBC's *Sherlock*, 2010-2017).

Set up next book

If you're writing a series, the last scenes are a great opportunity to set up interest for your next book. Perhaps your sleuth is adapting to a change: different job, change in title, a new boss, or a new partner. If you're writing a cozy, your sleuth may decide to stay in town and in the last paragraph of your book, a new potential villain walks through the door to her bookstore.

Establish the expectation that there is more to come, more change, more mysteries.

New normal

When the book opened, your character's normal world was disrupted in some way. They've spent however many chapters responding to your evil plot twists and unexpected insights. Not every sleuth will have a full character arc in every book, especially in novellas or series, but your sleuth has changed. The setting of the book has changed as a result of the crime and due to the loss of the victim, and possibly the villain.

What is the sleuth going to do now? Who will fill the shoes of the victim and villain? How has your world changed?

Final image

Leave your reader a final image that reflects the opening of your story. It can be a reversed image, a fun house image, but it should circle back in some way for a sense of completion.

It could be as simple as the detective getting another call or once again ordering their breakfast through the drive thru. For the amateur sleuth, they are diving back into their real job: writing, baking cookies, or arranging flowers.

The *Covert Affairs* (2010-2014) episode, *Walter's Walk*, opens with the sleuth refusing her sister's request to sign a paper for their family. During the episode, the sleuth comes to realize that family is more important than her job. In the ending image, she hands her sister the signed document.

The final image will inform whether the sleuth remains essentially unchanged, or if they are forever altered.

EXTRAS

MYSTERY BEAT SHEET

This summary of the acts and their beats can be useful for outlining, synopsis, plot analysis, or party planning. Okay, not party planning, unless it's one of those Murder Mystery Dinner parties. But no matter what tools you use to write—Scrivener, Word, 3x5 note cards, a spiral notebook—it's good to have an overview in mind. Even for an exploratory author who lets the story develop as they write, it can be useful to have a general idea of what needs to happen when. In a novella, you might have a chapter for each beat; in a novel, several chapters; in a short story, a scene. But this is the scaffold on which you will build your mystery.

———

Act 1: Setup
Introduce Sleuth and the World
Expose the Crime
Reactions and Complications
Undertaking the Investigation

Act 2: Fumbling
Investigations and Interrogations
Develop the Sleuth
Motives and Lies
Dire Disruption

Act 3: Connecting
Stonewalled
Missteps
Whittle Suspects
Fast Fail

Act 4: Solution
Reevaluate
Revelation
Final Battle
Resolution

THE MYSTERY DICTIONARY

Alibi: Proof that a suspect couldn't have committed the crime.

Beats: Interconnected structural elements of a genre. All the beats, universal or genre specific, must be in the story for it to *work*.

Buried Box Kidnapping: A victim is locked away in a fatal situation if not rescued in time, frequently in a box that is buried, with limited fundamental resources: air, food, water.

Clues: Information that helps solve the crime.

Chekhov's Gun: "One must not put a loaded rifle on the stage if one is not thinking of firing it." Anton Chekhov, Russian playwright. Or, to paraphrase, *don't screw with your readers*.

Coincidence: A remarkable party in which events that have never met before and are completely unrelated gather together to create a convenient plot point.

Deus Ex Machina: A contrivance that miraculously

saves the writer's plot bacon. The actual translation from the Greek is "god from the machinery."

Evidence: (1) Direct evidence is a fact based on a person's direct knowledge. The witness saw the murderer stab the victim with the knife. The bank teller identified the man who robbed her in a line up. No refutation, no inference, no other interpretation needed. (2) Indirect or circumstantial evidence is evidence that implies a person did the crime: fingerprints at the scene, the victim's blood in the defendant's car, tire tracks in the mud that match the suspect's car. Sleuths must then deduce what this means. For example, the fingerprints of the suspect might be at the crime scene because she's the victim's roommate.

Hunch: A guess, usually by the sleuth or someone associated with solving the crime, that isn't based on fact or evidence or clues, but on intuition and experience. But BEWARE. While it's a great way to move the plot over bumps, hunches should NOT drive the story.

Investigation: The actions taken by the sleuth(s) to uncover the details of a crime including the motive. It's important to note the word action. Your sleuth should be doing something: going to scenes, questioning people, talking to experts, performing experiments, or whatever it is going to take to figure out the mystery.

MacGuffin: Something that embodies the culprits' reasons for instigating the mystery. It's the driving emotional force of the story.

Maslow's Hierarchy of Needs: A psychological theory

of human needs based on five levels from food and shelter to self-actualization.

Means: The physical tools and abilities to commit the crime.

Motive: The reason the crime was committed.

Nosy Parker: A person who sticks their nose in everyone else's business, aka the perfect amateur sleuth.

Opportunity: Circumstance that make it possible to commit the crime.

POV: Point of view. The character who is acting as the narrator.

Primary Mystery: The question driving the plot of the story.

Red Herrings: False leads and irrelevant clues that point the detective and the reader toward the wrong solution to the mystery.

Series: A related collection of stories that have the same POV character(s) narrating the stories.

Sleuth: The person or people solving the primary mystery.

Smoking Gun: A seemingly conclusive and incontrovertible clue that identifies the culprit. Or does it?

Stakes: The compelling reasons for the actions the sleuth and the villain take.

Subplot: A story line that is secondary to the main story.

Suspect: Character(s) in the story who may have had means, motive, and/or opportunity to commit the crime.

Victim: The person who was robbed, kidnapped, killed, or experienced the specific crime of the primary mystery.

Villain: The person or people who instigated the crime in the primary mystery.

Witness: A character who may have seen or heard something related to the crime or has evidence related to the crime.

MYSTERY SUBGENRES

Just like romance novels, mystery novels come in many varieties. There are expectations within each subgenre. We aren't providing an exhaustive list. But you should get familiar with the expectations of the subgenre you're writing in. No matter which one it is—the beats apply.

Butler/British House Party mysteries are notable for their isolated setting and elite group of suspects. The country manor where many of these mysteries were set initially gave the subgenre its name, but islands, boats, and, of course, trains have also been used.

Capers/Heists focus on the villains as the protagonists, usually a team of them with a mastermind. Capers are committed by amateurs and heists involve professionals.

Cozy mysteries are populated by amateur sleuths who solve crimes more by using their special skills, intuition, and instinct, rather than by forensics or police procedures.

Hard-boiled/Modern PI has a detective that is tough as nails. The story will be grittier than a cozy and typically takes place in the urban underbelly of an American city. The detective can be a white-knight type or the antihero who isn't that far different from the criminal.

Historical mysteries are unique because the forensics are limited, and the cultural rules can be used as plot points.

Medical mysteries leverage the illness as the crime and the villain is the mysterious thing that caused the medical issue. There is an expectation of a tremendous amount of technical knowledge.

Legal mysteries involve officers of the court, including lawyers and law students and law clerks. Like medical and police procedurals, the legal details must be accurate.

Police procedurals focus will be on the detective or detectives and their investigation techniques. Forensics will be critical to the solution.

Speculative mysteries include alternate worlds, time travel, science fiction, and fantasy settings.

***

If you enjoyed this book...

Authors live for honest reviews. They help other readers find their books in a world where millions of books are published each year. So if you enjoyed this book and have just five minutes, leave a quick review at Amazon, Barnes and Noble, Kobo, Google, or even on our website...

Short or long, your words can make all the difference.

Thank you.

RedReines.com—sign up for the newsletter and get access to bonus content including the Demystifying the Beats Scrivener template.

Instagram: https://www.instagram.com/theredreines/
Facebook: https://www.facebook.com/theredreines

Dedicated to Gwen Hayes

Since we also write romance, we devoured Gwen Hayes's Romancing the Beat (2016), and wondered why there isn't something as pithy, helpful, and irreverent out there for mystery writers. (We checked. There isn't.) Thank you for inspiring us.

HEARTS OF THE MISSING - CHAPTER 1

HEARTS OF THE MISSING

By Carol Potenza

T siba'ashi D'yini Indian Reservation
New Mexico, USA

The harsh scrape, out of place in the quiet of predawn, penetrated the low buzz of the refrigeration motors. Like fingernails on a chalkboard, the sound made the hair on her neck and arms stand on end.

She wasn't alone anymore.

Her eyes narrowed as she peered through the open door of the office and into the cavernous space on the other side. Other than a few emergency lights pooling eerily on the floor, the room was dark, its bulky shelves and racks rising out of the linoleum like misshapen boulders.

Sergeant. Nicky Matthews was careful to make no sound as she placed her fingerprint brush on the metal shelf in front of her. She stripped off her latex gloves with quiet efficiency as she rose, dropping them on the floor by her feet. Her head cocked to the side, and she strained to hear any other sound that would indicate who—or how many—were just outside the broken plate-glass window of the mini-mart.

She hadn't heard a car pass by since she'd been here, and she'd sent the manager home after he'd let her inside.

Her police unit was parked in plain sight by the gas pumps, illuminated by the fluorescent lights in the metal canopy above it. Those lights formed a harsh bubble of white in the nighttime blackness that surrounded the building. The village store sat alone on a two-lane road, the only place to purchase food and gas for twenty miles in every direction. Porch lights from widely scattered trailers and small houses dotted the landscape, but she'd seen no one when she'd arrived. She'd been inside, processing the scene for over an hour. If the perps had come back, they must know she was here.

Another stealthy rasp, outside and to the left of the window.

She stiffened, focus shifting, tightening. Her hand slipped to her holster, palm scraping the butt of her

Glock 23. Whoever was out there was on the other side of the wall where she stood. She'd trained her phone's camera on that area earlier. The perps had used a bat or crowbar to bash in the large windows, and glass was strewn over the front sidewalk. At least one of them had cut themselves when they climbed inside. There were drops and smears of blood throughout the interior. She'd already gathered some samples for DNA testing, but the bloody smears turned into distinct prints in the office. One of the burglars spent quite a bit of time here, and that was where she'd been concentrating her efforts. But no longer.

Whoever was skulking outside had her full attention.

Nicky stepped forward, avoiding the half a dozen sunglasses knocked to the floor during the break-in. She turned her back to the wall, body coiled, and scanned the interior of the store for a change in the vague fluorescent light filtering into the room. Someone peering through the window would throw a shadow.

Her scalp prickled and a flash of heat swept over her skin. She swore she could feel a presence out there.

Waiting for her.

She drew in a slow breath, pulled her weapon, and pointed it down along her leg. Her finger rested across the trigger guard. She sidled closer to the window. Shards of glass littered the floor. The rubber soles of her boots muffled the crunch, but the sound was loud enough to make her wince. She paused, listening.

Seconds ticked by.

Nothing. No sound except the ever-present hum of the glass-doored coolers lining the back wall of the store.

She stayed in the shadows, her sharp gaze sweeping the gravel expanse of the parking lot. Tall, scraggly grass stood unmoving at the edge of the light. There was no wind, no scuttling leaves to explain away the noise.

Another minute passed. The feeling of a presence was fading. Nicky exhaled slowly. Her shoulders relaxed the tiniest bit, even as her expression twisted in faint confusion.

Had she been mistaken?

A movement caught her eye between the gas pumps, and she snapped her head to the right. Her body tensed. At a flash of color, Nicky stepped out of the shadows, not worried about the sound of scattering glass as she tracked the motion of...

A skinny brown rez dog wandered around the side of her unit, nose to the ground. Lifting its head, it sniffed the air. It trotted toward an overflowing trashcan and rose up on its hind feet, one front paw positioned delicately against the side. Nicky's lips pressed tight. You could count the ribs on that poor animal. Most likely it was a stray, but you never knew. It might belong to anyone in the village.

Relieved she had an answer to the sounds, Nicky holstered her pistol. Suddenly tired, she stretched, arching her back. Outside, the sky was beginning to gray. She checked the clock on the wall above the door. The sun would be up in a few minutes, and it would still take another hour to process the crime scene. Then she was going to canvass the nearest homes, to see if anyone had heard or seen anything. She probably wouldn't be done until hours after her shift was officially over.

Her gaze focused closer, and she stared at the pale oval of her reflection in what was left of the glass window in front of her. Dark brown eyes stared back as she ran her hand over the top of her head and slid her fingers through the smooth, straight black hair of her ponytail. She was mistaken for Native all the time. Not by Indians—but by the non-Indians she encountered on the reservation and at the casino.

She sighed deeply, glanced at the dog one more time, and froze. A wave of unease washed over her, this time prickling up her back. The animal stared at the front of the store, fixated, not on the place where she stood, but to the left of the window's edge.

At the place she'd first heard the noise.

Her hand dropped to her sidearm and Nicky jerked her head around. An old Native woman stared at her through the glass.

No. Not through the glass. In the glass.

The old woman's face was *in the glass*.

Their eyes met, and every nerve in Nicky's body stretched taut. The woman's pupils glowed black, glittering and alive, sharp points embedded within a deeply wrinkled face. An ancient, disembodied face.

Nicky *knew* she was supposed to look away—had been told in no uncertain terms by her traditional friends on the rez, but she couldn't move. She was transfixed.

The sun flashed over the horizon, blinding her.

But not before the woman smiled and turned away. Her long white hair whipped in the light—and she was gone.

Nicky yanked out her gun, hit the front door of the mini-mart hard and ran outside into the brightness of dawn, skidding on the broken glass. The same scraping sound that had alerted her only a few minutes before grated along her skin.

A flash of white raced away and her arms swung up, the muzzle of her sidearm tracking a rabbit as it zigged and zagged out of the parking lot, across the road and into the grass next to a trampled dirt path. She caught another movement out of the corner of her eye and her head swiveled to the dog. It cringed and shivered as it stared after the rabbit, before it backed up and loped away through the brush, tail tight between its legs.

Nicky's flesh crawled with goosebumps. Heart thudding, she pointed her weapon to the ground, clutching its diamond-patterned grip so tightly it cut deep into the skin of her palm.

Dammit, dammit, dammit!

Scowling, she slammed her weapon back into its holster.

The old woman was back.

That meant life was about to get complicated—and a lot more dangerous.

DIRTY DAISY - CHAPTER 1

DIRTY DAISY

By Jordyn Kross

Pain shot up Mikaela Mitchell's leg, and she crumpled onto the hot, middle-of-nowhere Texas highway. The slide and slam of the VW bus door clanged in her head like a TV jail cell. Her eyes stung and watered from the smoking tires, not from losing the only lead she had in her brother's death. Rolling up like an armadillo to minimize contact with the broiling asphalt, she dropped her head to her arms, which were wrapped around the bag the bastards had so kindly chucked out after her.

Despair burned almost as much as the road snot she'd landed in. She tugged at her borrowed, too-short white shorts. The nasty tar seeped into the fabric, ruining them forever. Around her, there was nothing but brambles and grasses, threatening to reclaim the paved-over land. Farther back, cicadas buzzed in clumps of trees standing in silent witness to her downfall. The red van barreled down the road, shrinking along with her options.

Shit. What good were journalistic skills without anyone to interview?

She dug in the roomy satchel she'd saved from crash-landing and retrieved her phone.

No signal.

No surprise.

Lifting her leg, she inspected her ankle—swelling fast. It screamed in protest when she tried to move it. She never should have let herself be talked out of flip-flops and into the fucked-up platform espadrilles. Sandals shouldn't have heels.

The late afternoon summer sun beat down, slow cooking her like BBQ ribs in an oil drum smoker. If she didn't figure out how to move—soon, and in what direction—she was dead. The only question was *how* she'd meet her doom? Dehydration? Hungry critter? Exsanguination from killer mosquitos? And since she was supposed to be gone all weekend under the guise of doing research for a travel article, it would be days before her roommate and best friend, Heather, noticed Mikaela missing. She dug into the asphalt with her good foot, inching her way toward safety.

A distant hum teased the air. Peering in the direction

she'd come from, a small black speck emerged through the haze. A vibration rattled up from the road, shaking her bones. Mikaela scooched again, moving about as fast as a pregnant tortoise but desperate to avoid being added to the goo.

A lethal, matte-metal machine pounded into focus before she'd covered half the distance to the edge. No way would she make it. She waved her arms, but the rider, covered head to boot in black, raced toward her like a demon released from hell. *Fuck.*

She could see the headline: *"Trollop Turned to Tar on Texas Trail."*

She squeezed her eyes closed and braced for impact.

Nothing.

She raised one eyelid. The front tire had burned to a stop inches from her bare thigh. Huffing out a breath, she opened her mouth to rail at the asshole about the dangerous stunt and then froze, taking in a mountain of leather.

The biker dropped the kickstand and leaned the silenced machine to the side. He lifted his beefy leg over the seat, lug sole boot dropping like a boulder to the ground. He—for there was no mistaking that monster as anything but male—stalked toward her. A full helmet with a mirrored visor hid his face. Her reflection was a wounded rabbit in the presence of the big, bad wolf. At least she hadn't screamed—her pride remained intact.

The beast scooped her up and silently strode back to his metal horse. He released her onto the seat, and she hastily slung the strap of her bag across her body. Then he straddled the seat in front of her, pushing her legs wide, knocking the stand back with his heel, and tilting the bike back to center. The mechanical pulse rumbled through her core as she flailed to find purchase for her feet, losing one of the cursed espadrilles in the process. He grabbed her left arm and tugged it around his waist to the rock wall of his abdomen.

Mikaela shut down any protest and snapped her other arm around him as they rocketed in the same direction the damn van had gone. A ride was a ride when abandoned to the vultures.

There. Up ahead. The red VW was turning.

She beat on the behemoth's back. "Follow them! I have to—"

A bug flew down her throat, and she gagged on its bendy legs and the juicy body while they rode past where the distant van was kicking up dust on an unmarked trail. Mikaela pummeled the leather-covered back. She'd find that dirt road. And when she saw her dead brother's ex-girlfriend, Karla, again, she was going to throat punch that bitch.

———

Ryder Ruiz's personal code of honor wouldn't allow him to leave Roadkill Chick on the highway, but he wasn't any happier than she was about picking her up. A perfect solo test ride of his just-out-of-the-shop dream interrupted by a scantily clad, leggy brunette might be some other guy's idea of luck, but for Ryder it was a pain in his ass. There was no cell signal that far from Daisy, so the only option was to carry her back to town. If she couldn't solve her problems with a phone call, he could dump her with the sheriff. His cousin would take care of her.

He pulled into the driveway of his mechanic shop and retrieved the remote for the first bay door from his jacket pocket. It cranked open, and he guided his baby back inside. He turned off the engine and lifted himself off the seat. Roadkill Girl didn't move except to put a bare foot down with an obvious wince.

Great.

He'd have to help her. After he tugged his helmet off, he shook out his long hair, releasing the heat and sweat. His helmet went on the nearby shelf before he returned to his bike. Her honey-brown eyes were wide and locked on him. Unable to help himself, he quirked an eyebrow and gave her a half grin.

She squirmed, ready to run when she couldn't even walk. He plucked her off the seat. She couldn't weigh but a buck twenty, buck thirty. He started to set her down, but she only had the one shoe, and her other ankle was the size of an orange. One glance at his motorcycle seat and he decided not to put her in his favorite chair either.

An ass print. In tar. On the brand-new leather.

He flipped the girl over his shoulder. *That* got her talking.

"Hey. You can't throw me around like a sack of potatoes. I don't care how pretty you are. Where the hell am I anyway, and why didn't you follow that van?"

Van? Nobody else had been on the road. And he damn well wasn't *pretty*.

He grabbed a shop rag and draped it over the top of a stool before placing her admittedly sweet backside on it. "Someone you can call?"

"That's it? No introduction or explanation?" She dropped her face into a doltish mask and lowered her voice. "*Someone you can call?*"

"Not interested in your name." No matter how sassy and attractive he found her. "*You* were on the side of the road. *You* know why. And *you* need to call someone." He held out his cell.

She pulled a phone out of her bag, ignoring his. Ryder tucked his cell back in his pocket and went to the storage cabinet to find something to remove the tar from his baby.

When he finally found a cleanser that might not ruin the seat, she was talking, but it was clear she was leaving a message for someone. Ryder resisted rolling his eyes. The road crap faded with some rubbing, but her ass was permanently branded on his bike. *Shit.*

"You got somewhere I can change?" Her voice was heavy like wood smoke, and it curled around him.

"Change?"

"I've got clothes in my bag, but a little privacy would be good. Then I won't get any more crap on your stuff." She tugged off her lone shoe and, with a perfectly aimed hook shot, sank it in his large metal waste bin.

"Basketball?" She had the legs for it.

"My brother liked to have someone to practice with

when we were growing up." She sniffed and turned her head.

"Bathroom's that way." Ryder pointed past the stairs that led to the entrance of his attached house.

She hopped a few steps.

Ryder picked her up and stomped to the guest bath. "Someone coming for you?"

"Uh. My roommate should be home soon." She swiped the hair off her face. "We live in Houston. I'm sure she'll check her messages anytime now."

He adjusted course, flipped her over his shoulder again, and took the stairs. It was too late in the day to ferry the chick all the way to Houston. It'd have to wait until morning.

As soon as he unlocked his door, Mow came over to serpentine through his legs.

"Who's this?" Roadkill Girl had pushed up off his back and was staring at his three-legged black cat.

"Mow."

"Mow," she purred. "I'm Mike."

Mike? Didn't quite capture the lush curves and long legs that screamed female. But then, *mud pie* didn't exactly capture the sweetness of that dessert either. Ryder set the girl, whose name he knew despite not wanting to, in front of the counter in his bathroom. "Take your time. There's Advil in the cabinet."

He shut the door behind him and checked Mow's kibble and water. Grabbing two glasses, he filled them with ice and added water from his filtered pitcher. The bathroom door opened, and Mike hobbled out, looking much more put together despite her injured foot. Black yoga pants, a t-shirt with a cartoon horse and rainbows, and her hair in a ponytail. She looked nothing like the vixen he'd scooped up. And her attractiveness multiplied. Ryder put his drink down and retrieved a bag of peas from the freezer while she planted herself in his chair.

He knelt in front of her. "Can you move your foot?"

"Kind of." She winced as she flexed it up and down.

"Any numbness or tingling?"

"I wish. Just pain."

"Can I check?" He held his hand over her foot.

She shrugged. "Go ahead."

He pressed down, but she didn't rear back. Probably not broken. He placed her foot on his coffee table and wrapped the frozen veg around her ankle.

"Thank you," she said.

Once she'd had some of the water and downed her pills, he sat on his couch across from the chair she was in. "So, what brings you to Daisy?"

"Is that where I am?"

Ryder waited. Given enough silence, most people talk. Mow jumped into Mike's lap and pressed kitty paws into her thighs while circling before curling up for a snooze. Mike studied the cat and stroked her long black fur. Huh. Mow didn't like people. She usually hid on the rare occasions Ryder had someone over.

"It was supposed to be a long weekend trip. With some friends. Well, not friends. My brother's ex-girlfriend. We've been hanging out lately, and she knows some guys with a boat and a cabin in the national forest." Mike shrugged one shoulder.

"Why were you on the road?"

"Oh, uh...Peter, the guy with the boat, he started getting handsy. When I told him no, the others laughed, called me a prude, and the guy who owns the van pulled over and said if I wasn't going to be any fun, I should get out. Then he pushed me out the door. Literally."

Ryder stared at Mike. She had more tells than an amateur poker player. And most of what she'd said had been true. But not all of it. Why lie to him? Didn't matter. "I'll give you a ride back to Houston in the morning if you don't hear from your roommate."

"I should probably get a hotel."

"Don't worry about it. You can hang out here." Maybe she'd tell him some more of the story. Because if there was something happening in his backyard, he needed to share it with his cousin. Donny wasn't the best sheriff, but he listened to Ryder. Besides, it was high season, and the only inn was probably booked.

"If I'm staying, can I at least get your name?" she asked.

Ryder stood and extended his hand. "Ryder Ruiz."

She placed her hand in his. A weird shot of electricity spiked up his arm.

"Mikaela Mitchell." Her smile hit him in the chest. "You can call me Mike."

ABOUT THE AUTHORS

Carol Potenza taught biochemistry at New Mexico State University before transitioning to a full-time mystery writer. Her first book was the Tony Hillerman Prize winner, Hearts of the Missing, followed by The Third Warrior and Spirit Daughters, the second and third book in the Nicky Matthews mystery. She writes two other mystery series: the De-extinct Zoo Mysteries, and the Lies series.

Carol loves the combination of strong women sleuths, paranormal and murder mystery, mixed with science or, as she likes to call it—BiocheMystery. She sets all her books in the beautiful state of New Mexico, where she lives with her husband, Leos, and her extremely grumpy chihuahua, Hermès.

To receive special offers, bonus content, and info on new releases and other great reads, sign up for her newsletter at www.carolpotenza.com

Jordyn Kross is an award-winning unapologetically naughty novelist who spent years honing her writing skills with tech manuals and marginal poetry before finding her passion for writing sexy, boundary-stretching happily-ever-afters.

When she's not writing, she's attempting to garden in the desert Southwest, hiking with her insane pound posse, and admiring that handsome man wandering around her house who continues to stay.

Jordyn enjoys saucy double entendres, pretending to be an extrovert, and is well-known for having no filter.

Her first carnal mystery (there's nothing cozy about it), Dirty Daisy, is available wherever ebooks are sold, and some shady back alleys.

Find out more at jordynkross.com

Ryley Banks writes award-winning and bestselling sexy romance, mostly of the LGBTQ+ variety. She's a connoisseur of tea and gin and loves language, especially creative profanity. When she's not begging her characters to behave or reading fanfic, you can find Ryley crafting the next story to make you smile and set you on fire. Stop by and say hi at: https://ryleybanks.com

For news, updates, freebies, and insider info, join Ryley's VIP newsletter!

Follow and say hi to Ryley on Instagram, Twitter, Facebook, Goodreads, and BookBub

Erin Krueger is a lover of all things historic, from her framed 1810 Ackerman's repository fashion plate hung in her office to the 1940s magazines she has spread out in a radius from her desk chair. She's the author of seven stories spanning from the Regency period through to the present day, time-travel included, and has been an avid reader of mystery novels ever since she picked up her very first Nancy Drew as a child. Hooked by carefully woven plots and sneaky sleuths, there's always an element of intrigue or espionage in her works. As far as she knows, she's not related to the fiendish 80's villain with the same last name, but the DNA has yet to be processed. To find out more about her, pop over to erinkruegerwrites.com

For news, updates, freebies, and exclusive fun, join her newsletter!

Follow and pop over for a cozy chat with Erin on Instagram, Twitter, and Facebook.

ALSO BY THE AUTHORS

Carol Potenza

Hearts of the Missing: A Mystery

The Third Warrior: A Nicky Matthews Mystery

Spirit Daughters: A Nicky Matthews Mystery

Unmasked: A De-Extinct Zoo Mystery

Coming 2023

Sting of Lies

Jordyn Kross

Melting Hearts Series

Prequel Novella - Jack's Frost

(free for newsletter subscribers)

Book 1 - Winter's List

Book 2 - Xmas Angel

Book 3 - Shattered Ice

Dirty Daisy Mystery Series

Book 1 - Dirty Daisy

Book 2 - Coming Soon

Ryley Banks

Ink: Queer Sci Fi's Eighth Annual Flash Fiction Contest Anthology

Big Book of Orgasms: 69 Sexy Stories (Volume 2) Anthology

Tangled Destinies Series

Book 1 - Fate's Awakening - Coming Soon

Erin Krueger

Designers in Time Series

Book 1 - Khaki and Lace - A 1940s Historic Time Travel Romance - Coming Soon

ACKNOWLEDGMENTS

Carol: One of the joys in my life has been the three women who co-wrote this book with me. I can't tell you how much I appreciate their support, their critique of my work—they make my writing so much better—their truths, and when I need it, their prevarications. Thank you J.K., E.K., and R.B. I am so glad we decided to take part of this crazy publishing journey together.

Jordyn would like to thank the RR's, without whom the dream of being an author would still be just a dream. Her hubs for tolerating her wacky schedule, endless "research," and inappropriate humor. Her Insane Pound Posse for making sure she rose from her chair occasionally. And all the mystery authors who provided such a wealth of examples to draw from as we drafted this book.

Ryley would like to thank the RRs: JK, CP, and EK, who make the tastiest sausage; her husband B who, in addition to unwavering love and support, long ago learned a full stomach = happy author; her parents, N and C, for instilling a love of reading; and Mrs. O'B, for putting up with her reading Nancy Drew mysteries in the middle of class.

Erin would like to thank the RR's who've been the greatest source of support and critique possible, her mother P.B. with her enormous book horde that started the whole reading thing, Ms. Keene who gave her the hope of one day becoming her own version of Nancy Drew, her friend A.P. for introducing her to *Miss Fisher* back in 2013, C.P. and J.K. for their hard work and dedication to the mystery craft that drew her in, Acorn TV and Netflix services that brought countless mysteries into her home, Ms. Kowal for continuing her love of paranormal mystery through Ginger, and Ms. Freeman for all the late nights with Frances.

Made in the USA
Middletown, DE
03 November 2023

41931778R00076